# FAST JETS

# FAST JETS

## A pilot's eye view   Chris Allan

### Osprey Colour Series

Published in 1986 by Osprey Publishing Limited
27A Floral Street, London WC2E 9LP
Member company of the George Philip Group

British Library Cataloguing in Publication Data

Allan, Chris
    Fast jets: a pilot's eye view.—(Osprey colour series)
    1. Fighter planes—Pictorial works   2. Jet planes, Military—
    Pictorial works
    I. Title
    623.74'64   UG1242.F5

ISBN 0-85045-661-4

Editor Dennis Baldry
Designed by David Tarbutt
Printed in Italy

**Front cover** 'Shackling' into battle port with a
Sidewinder-armed Hawk T.1A. On the call 'shackle' the
leader and his No 2 change/swop formation to control
and exploit any change in the tactical situation. This
manoeuvre (the left-hand aircraft goes right, and vice-
versa) is potentially dangerous at low-level with well
camouflaged aircraft—a hazard aggravated by the need to
avoid 'ballooning' too high during the change-over and
losing the protective cloak of the surrounding terrain. It is
the responsibility of the No 2 to ensure safe separation
from the leader's aircraft

**Title pages** A self portrait of the author leading a US Air
Force F-15 Eagle into Deci

**Back cover** Detail of a *Luftwaffe* F-4F Phantom II of
JG-74 'Mölders' based at Neuberg

Lightning F.6 'Delta Foxtrot' was the photo-ship used for
most of the air-to-air shots in this book. The aircraft is
being flown by 'Fieldy' (Flt Lt Paul Field), and it bears the
name of Binbrook's OC operations, Wg Cdr Derek North.
Unusually, to enhance its role as a target for practice
interceptions, this particular Lightning features a 'hatch
pack' fuel cell in the ventral tank to gain an extra 800 lb
(363 kg) of JP4 at the expense of the standard twin 30
mm Aden gunpack

# Contents

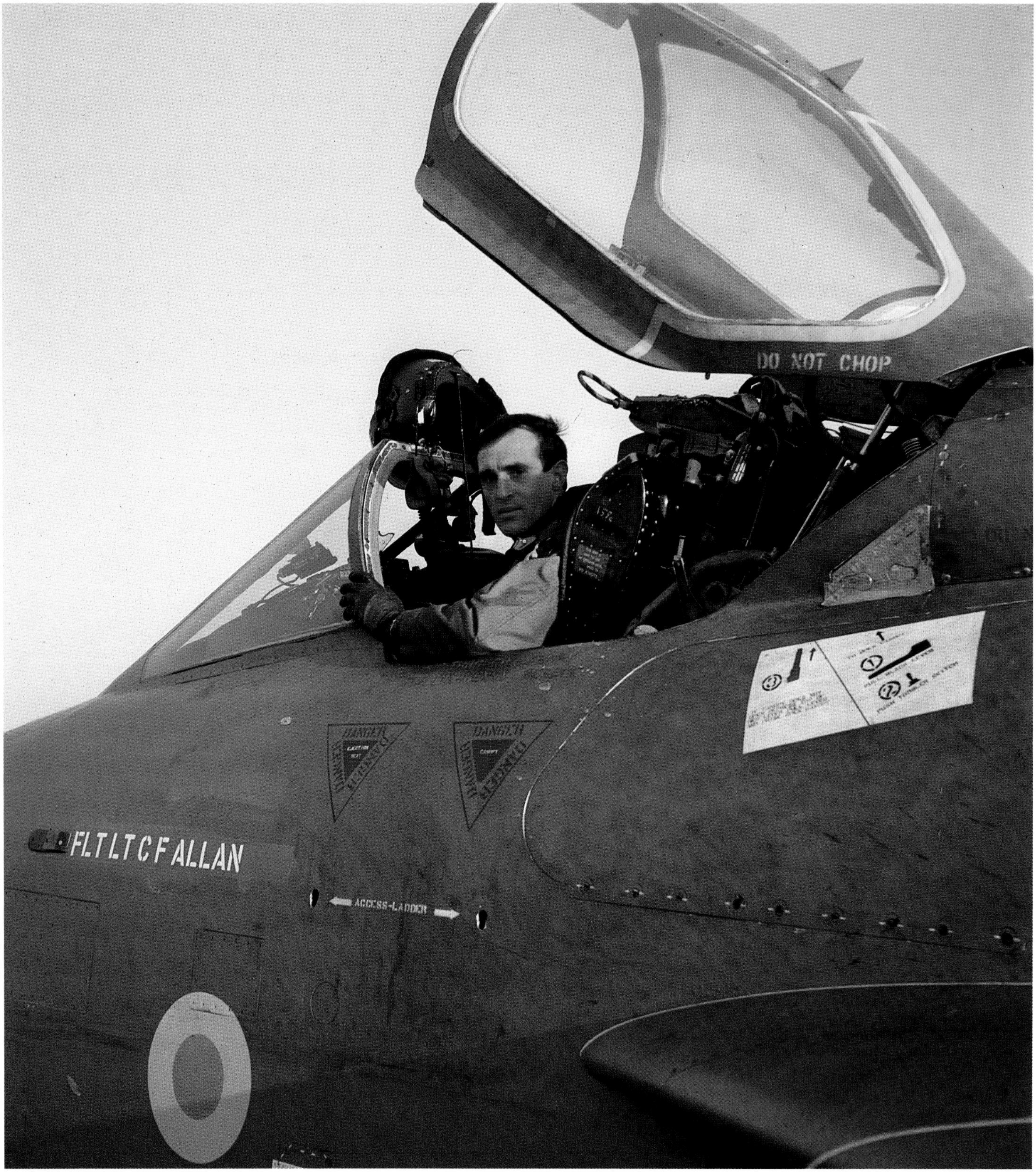
DO NOT CHOP
DANGER
DANGER
FLT LT C F ALLAN
ACCESS-LADDER

Flight Lieutenant Chris Allan (pictured in the cockpit of his Lightning F.3, 'Alpha Bravo') is an RAF pilot based at Binbrook in Lincolnshire. Interestingly, after gaining his Wings in 1978, he became the last student to qualify on the Folland Gnat advanced trainer.

He is currently a Qualified Weapons Instructor with the Lightning Training Flight (LTF), a unit tasked with training new pilots and weapons instructors for the RAF's last classic single-seat fighter. In sharp contrast to the skills involved in flying a Lightning, he intends to own and fly a Pitts Special aerobatic biplane. Aged 29, he lives close to Binbrook with his wife Lily and their young son Alexander.

This book would not have been possible without the generous help of many individuals. Lack of space makes it impossible to print the long list of names required, but the author is pleased to offer a collective 'thank you' to them all

*FAST JETS* was shot using Nikon and Rollei equipment loaded with Ektachrome and Kodachrome film. All of the air-to-air photographs were taken during normal training flights. The views expressed in this book are the author's and do not necessarily reflect those of the Ministry of Defence or of the Royal Air Force.

(Photo: Anthony Kirby, Group 3 Studios, Grimsby)

**To Thomo, Frosty, and Tetley.**

**They soared, like their hopes,**
**To seek and defend**
**Each man and machine**
**As one, to the end . . .**

*Maggie May*

# Making the grade

A study of Hawk T.1 XX315 of No 1 TWU at Brawdy in South Wales from the back seat of another Hawk during combat standardization training, an exercise designed to enable instructors to teach the art of air combat training (ACT). The Hawk is a superb aircraft and whenever they clash in a one-on-one engagement the combat usually becomes a fierce 7G turning fight at base height (5000 ft/1524 m); the fighting abilities of two experienced pilots cancel-out and the normal thrust-and-parry of air combat degenerates into a sweaty endurance test. At 7G the pilot's head and bonedome is the equivalent weight of an average man, so it's hardly surprising that many instructors at Brawdy (and at No 2 TWU at Chivenor in North Devon) find they need shirts with a larger neck after sampling the Hawk's 'fatiguing' manoeuvrability

Although many pilots think of the Jet Provost (JP) as a 'puddle jumper', it has served the RAF with distinction in the training role. It is sufficiently demanding to get the best out of a young student and instill the good habits that are essential in no-nonsense military flying. The JP is capable of comprehensive aerobatic sequences and it's ideal for building-up the confidence and experience of fast-jet candidates. This example, a T.5A, is based at the RAF College Cranwell

**Overleaf and above** Hawk T.1 XX159 of No 234 (shadow) Sqn flying a simulated attack profile (SAP) around Wales and Southeast England. Typically, an SAP sortie involves finding three separate ground targets and the 'attacks' are later evaluated by the squadron's weapons instructor to determine their accuracy and effectiveness. Flown by ex-Poachers display pilot Sqn Ldr Eddie Banks, this Hawk is armed with a centreline 30 mm Aden cannon pod

**Above right** Flt Lt Andy Carolyn flying Hawk XX315 at low-level over the jagged coastline of Pembrokeshire

**Right** Hawk XX159 over the ogin on its way back to Brawdy

The air defence grey colour scheme of this Hawk T.1A of
No 151 (shadow) Sqn from No 2 TWU at Chivenor is
best suited to operations at medium level. Even darker
'Indian' greys (so-called because the scheme was
introduced on Indian Navy Sea Harriers) are now in
operational use—the darker greys applied to Royal Navy
Sea Harriers during the Falklands conflict were found to
be more protective. This aircraft is fitted with two
Sidewinder acquisition rounds on the underwing pylons

**Above** A crisp break by Hawk T.1A XX200, crewed by Flt Lts Mike Philips and Neil Rodgers

**Right** Hawk with talons: in wartime the Hawk TWUs would be tasked with the low-level defence of Britain's key airfields and other important installations. Operating in a 'high/low mix' with Tornado F.3s and F-4s, the Hawk is likely to bring a deep penetration by an enemy interdictor/strike aircraft to a terminal conclusion with an AIM-9L Sidewinder

A Brawdy-bound Hawk is almost silhouetted against an ethereal backdrop. Flt Lt Maurice 'Spike' Newbery piloted the photo-ship Hawk

The outstanding visibility from the rear cockpit makes the Hawk ideal for weapons instruction. This view, taken moving into line astern behind another Hawk, also illustrates the MDC (miniature detonating cord) which shatters the canopy at the start of the ejection sequence, and the Ferranti ISIS F.195R gyro gunsight used for air-to-air/air-to-ground aiming

21

# Mud-movers

A Jaguar T.2 of No 226 OCU based at Lossiemouth en route, low down, to attack targets in 'Moon country'—the northern part of Scotland where the population density is the lowest in Europe. The Jaguar officially entered RAF service in June 1974 and by the late seventies the type equipped eight squadrons, plus an OCU. But by the beginning of 1986 the number of Jaguar squadrons had been halved with almost indecent haste in favour of the Tornado GR.1

RUBIC lead and his No 2 departing Binbrook, 20 seconds ahead from brakes off of 3 and 4. When these pictures were taken in August 1985, No 14 was the last single-seat strike/attack squadron in the RAF; this unit has now converted to the Tornado GR.1 but it is still based at Brüggen in West Germany. The Smiths HUD (head-up display) is presenting (clockwise) speed in knots, magnetic heading, angle of attack (AOA), and height information

**Below** RUBIC 4, (XX746/'AB') cleaned-up, 'burner's in. The Lightning QRA (quick reaction alert) shed is directly below

**Above** On this Mallet Blow exercise the Jags carried a pair of 264 Imp gal (1200 lit) fuel tanks underwing and a centreline CBLS (carrier bomb light stores) armed with four, 4 kg practice bombs

RUBIC Flight at low-level in echelon starboard, 15 miles off the south coast holiday resort of Bournemouth in Dorset. Shortly after this photograph was taken, bad weather forced the four-ship to fly in individual pairs and pull up to 'Victor Mike' and proceed in VFR/VMC (visual flight rules/visual meteorological conditions)

**Above right** The Jaguar is difficult to spot at low-level where its camouflage and small size combine to frustrate a visual pick-up by predatory air defence pilots. Unfortunately, it has a very bright anti-collision light on the fuselage spine which is an obvious handicap—in wartime the light would be switched off . . .

26

Twisting down the valleys of northwest Scotland, the
pilot of this Jaguar T.2 is only too well aware that he
could soon find a Lightning or Phantom driver sniffing at
his six, closing-in for the kill. Evasive manoeuvring
presents a real challenge because the Jag is not over-
endowed with specific excess power (SEP), and it has a
restrictive AOA limit. The standard tactic is to accelerate,
descend to base height (250 ft/75 m), and jink, bunt, and
weave for all you're worth

**Above** A two-tone grey Northrop F-5A (K-3046) of No 316 Sqn, Royal Netherlands Air Force, at Binbrook in July 1985 during a NATO exchange with the Lightnings of No 5(F) Sqn

**Above right** Taxying out to runway 03 at Binbrook: Dutch F-5 pilots train for the air-to-air role, but the main emphasis is placed on ground attack. The RNAF acquired its F-5s in the late sixties with American assistance and the type is expected to remain in the inventory until 1995

Stay cool. . .

**Left** After a dissimilar air combat sortie against a flight of Lightnings, Leek and Boss get their story straight before the all-important debrief. Weapons instructors decide 'who got who' by analyzing gun camera film and data from missile attack recorders. Claims are discounted if a pilot fails to achieve the correct 'angle-off', or fires before the target is in range. The F-5 packs a pair of Colt M-39 20 mm cannons in the nose: each gun has 280 rounds belt-fed from magazines underneath the gun bays

A tunnel of open Harrier canopies lead the way to Flt Lt Nick Gilchrist, RAF Germany Harrier display pilot in 1985 and a QWI with No 4 Sqn based at Gütersloh. During the Falklands conflict in 1982, Gilchrist took off from Ascension Island at the controls of a Harrier GR.3 and landed on the carrier HMS *Hermes* after being airborne for 8 hours 25 minutes

A Martin-Baker Mk 9B ejection seat in the front cockpit of a Harrier T.4. The 9B is an extremely capable zero-zero seat, but an engine failure in the hover is still quite a lot of bovver—pilots have only a split second to pull the handle before impact

The stubby snout of a Harrier T.4 of No 233 OCU probes the morning air. Like the single-seat GR.3, the trainer is equipped with a Ferranti laser ranger and marked target seeker (LRMTS) in the nose

**Above** A Welsh wild cat adorns the squadron crest of
No 233 OCU. The OCU was formed in 1952 at
Pembrey in South Wales as a Hunter conversion unit and
re-equipped with the Harrier in 1970

**Preceding pages** The Harrier was the world's first
operational V/STOL combat aircraft (No 1(F) Sqn,
Wittering, 1969) and it remains the most survivable
fixed-wing asset in the RAF's inventory. It is also the
only current RAF front-line combat aircraft to have been
involved in a shooting war—the 1982 showdown in the
South Atlantic. This was the first time this particular pilot
had graduated from 'press ups' (vertical take offs and
landings on the same spot), to landing amid the trees
around Wittering. I'm glad he touched down on the right
spot

**Left** Although this No 1(F) Sqn Harrier GR.3 is concealed
under camouflage netting at a dispersed site at Wittering,
it would be equally happy lurking in a forest hide or
underground car park. The PSP matting under its main
gear and outriggers stops the aircraft sinking into wet
ground

Flt Lt Jeff Glover's Harrier T.4 being brought to cockpit readiness by Sqn Ldr 'Chris' Gowers during hide training at Wittering in 1985. A groundcrew respirator dangles on the aircraft's ladder, at hand to simulate the spectre of NBC (nuclear/biological/chemical) attack in war; disruptive pattern dress is worn to avoid wear and tear on the expensive charcoal lining fitted to a real NBC suit.

Flt Lt Glover was shot down on his first mission in the Falklands war by 20 mm AAA (anti-aircraft artillery), his GR.3 crashing near Port Howard. His parachute did not deploy fully and he sustained serious injuries. He was captured by Argentine troops and flown to a military hospital at Comodoro Rivadavia on the Argentine mainland and was subsequently repatriated to Britain after the cessation of hostilities

Leaving its shadow on the ground, a Harrier GR.3 of No 1(F) Sqn flies at low-level during a recce mission. The pilot must negotiate simulated engagement zones and 'safe' areas to 'get the pictures' (an F.95 camera is located in the nose, pointing to port) and/or relay position reports on the disposition and strength of 'enemy' ground forces. To make exercises like this more realistic, inflatable mock-up tanks and personnel carriers are used to simulate Soviet armour

**Overleaf** This close-up gives a good view of the squadron badge; their motto is *In omnibus princeps*— foremost in everything. The yaw vane in front of the armour-glass windshield is also clearly visible; it indicates wind direction when the aircraft is moving at slow speed, particularly useful during the transition from forward flight to the hover

Flt Lt Jim Fernie is pushed back into Hide 3 at Osnabrück airfield in April 1985, when the Harrier's of No 4 Sqn were deployed away from their normal operating base at Gütersloh to get some practice 'in the field'. When concealment is complete the pilot is debriefed in the cockpit via a telebrief connector plugged-in to the aircraft; during turnround he is also briefed for the next sortie

**Below, right and overleaf** TANGO 301, a Buccaneer
S.2B (XT283/'GC') of No 237 OCU from Lossie, piloted
by F/O Trevor Beadle with staff navigator Flt Lt John
Bennett in the back seat, tracking over North Wales on
its way to an Open Day at RAF Abingdon in September
1985. It was my lucky day. I too was bound for the
static display park at the same event, so I saved myself
the trouble of finding the place by tagging along in my
Lightning all the way to Abingdon. I let the nav do all
the work—no hard feelings, John!

Despite the introduction of Tornado, two squadrons of
Buccaneers (Nos 12 and 208) are being retained in the
maritime strike role; both units are now equipped with
the advanced Sea Eagle anti-ship missile

Engine change for a Warthog: after diverting to Binbrook, this A-10 was fitted with a replacement TF34 turbofan in six hours. Normally, an engine change for a front-line combat aircraft is measured in days. The name Warthog is unofficial but it seems to have stuck—it's less cumbersome than Thunderbolt II.

A mean, slab-sided hunk, the A-10 is designed around a massive seven-barrel GAU-8/A Avenger cannon—a gun capable of demolishing a main battle tank with a short squirt of 30 mm shells (1 second equals 70 rounds); lethality is enhanced by the depleted uranium penetrators in the ammo. MiG-drivers take note: the gun is capable of air-to-air kills out to 1400 yards (1280 m).

Although a hog by name, it's not by nature, being reluctant to bite the hand that flies it. The A-10s fine handling qualities are appreciated by pilots who fly it down to 50 ft (15 m) at 350 knots (560 km/h), relying on terrain masking, a heavy punch, and the aircraft's survivability features to complete the mission

A-7D Corsair II of the 125th Tactical Fighter Squadron, 138th Tactical Fighter Group, Oklahoma Air National Guard, sits on the tarmac during an overseas deployment to RAF Wittering in 1985. Teamed with Harriers of No 1(F) Sqn, the Tulsa-based part-timers impressed everyone with their slick professionalism

Prior to energizing the A-7s TF41 turbofan (license-built Rolls-Royce Spey), an ANG pilot goes through the checklist. He wears the new HGU-55/P lightweight helmet

A SLUF (short little ugly 'fella') is serviced alongside a Harrier T.4 by ANG groundcrew

The deep, gaping intake is characteristic of the SLUF; directly underneath it is a Pave Penny laser target locator. AN/APQ-126(V) Doppler radar is mounted in the nose, providing air-to-ground ranging, terrain-following, and terrain-avoidance data. The unit badge near the cockpit is a muscrat holding a hand of cards—an ace, deuce, and a five (125). Neat

The 125th use a standardized lizard-green 'Europe One'
paint scheme with low-viz national markings and codes

The cockpit of the A-7 is one of the best equipped in the
business—not bad for 'weekend warriors'. Key features
include the HUD and a PMDS (projected map display set)

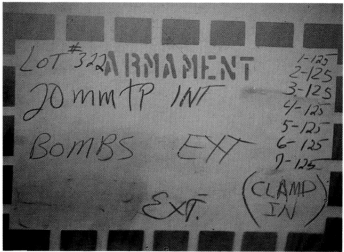

ARMAMENT
LOT #322
20 mm TP INT
BOMBS EXT
EXT (CLAMP IN)

1-125
2-125
3-125
4-125
5-125
6-125
7-125

U.S. AIR FORCE

**Left** A-7 wing station loaded with practice bombs. The bombs are locked in place by flagged pins for pre-flight safety

**Below left** The 125th use a code to log the weapon load carried by the aircraft. Lot Nos of shells, calibre, and the number of successive load-ups are recorded; irregular figures indicate a failure to 'fire out', which probably points to a gun fault. The A-7D is fitted with a 20 mm Vulcan M61A1 six-barrel cannon with 1000 rounds

**Above** The final A-7 built (delivered in September 1984) was a two-seat A-7K. Every A-7 unit in the Guard has one of these rare birds for conversion training

Without air-to-air refuelling (AAR), US Air Force and ANG units would be unable to rapidly reinforce NATO air power in an emergency. The 125th TFS deployed to Wittering in 9 hours 15 minutes by refuelling from KC-135A and KC-10A tankers. **Below** A KC-135 tops up from a KC-10 Extender en route. **Overleaf** Dwarfed by a KC-10, an A-7 gulps JP4 from the tanker's flying boom

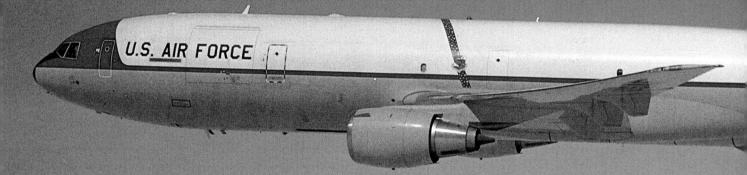

# Deci

On the ramp at Decimomannu, Sardinia, in June 1985: a Tornado from JaboG 32, West German Air Force (*Bundes Luftwaffe*), basks in Italian sunshine prior to a bombing mission on the range. Having replaced the F-104G Starfighter, Tornado is the primary battlefield interdiction, close air support, and counter air asset in the *Luftwaffe*

**Above** Tornado totes a pair of 27 mm Mauser cannons (reduced to one in the air defence F.3) for ground straffing and self-protection. Armourers push back the gun barrels after routine servicing

Graduated markings on the wing show the sweep angles, used during mensuration checks to confirm the symmetry of the airframe. Any distortion would indicate that the aircraft had been overstressed

**Left** Unloading 4 kg practice bombs to arm each Tornado on the line

The Tornados variable geometry wing varies in sweep from 25 to 67 degrees

**Below left** Armourers locate the practice bombs into centreline canisters

**Below** Two of the Tornado four-ship on the way to the range. The reflection is from the pilot's helmet

Tornados on the line: West Germany is acquiring 112 for the *Marineflieger* and 212 for the *Luftwaffe*

A Harrier GR.3 of No 4 Sqn stands ready for another load of practice bombs, plus re-load rounds for its two 30 mm Aden cannons

Under the searing heat of Sardinian sunshine, a tactical brolley keeps the cockpit relatively cool and bearable. The pennant on the nose confirms that this Harrier is the mount of Wg Cdr P. V. Harris, Boss of No 4 Sqn

**Left and above** Collecting a half-load of 30 mm shells (120 rounds per Aden) and preparing them for eventual 'canning' into the ammo tank

**Right** Sgt Orme gets into his stride with a couple of 4 kg practice bombs

**Far right** Sunrise at Deci heralds another day of intensive flying; the reliability of the weather guarantees high sortie rates. A Harrier catches the first rays of the day

**Below** Flight Systems Incorporated usually have three TF-100F Super Sabres at Deci for target towing duties

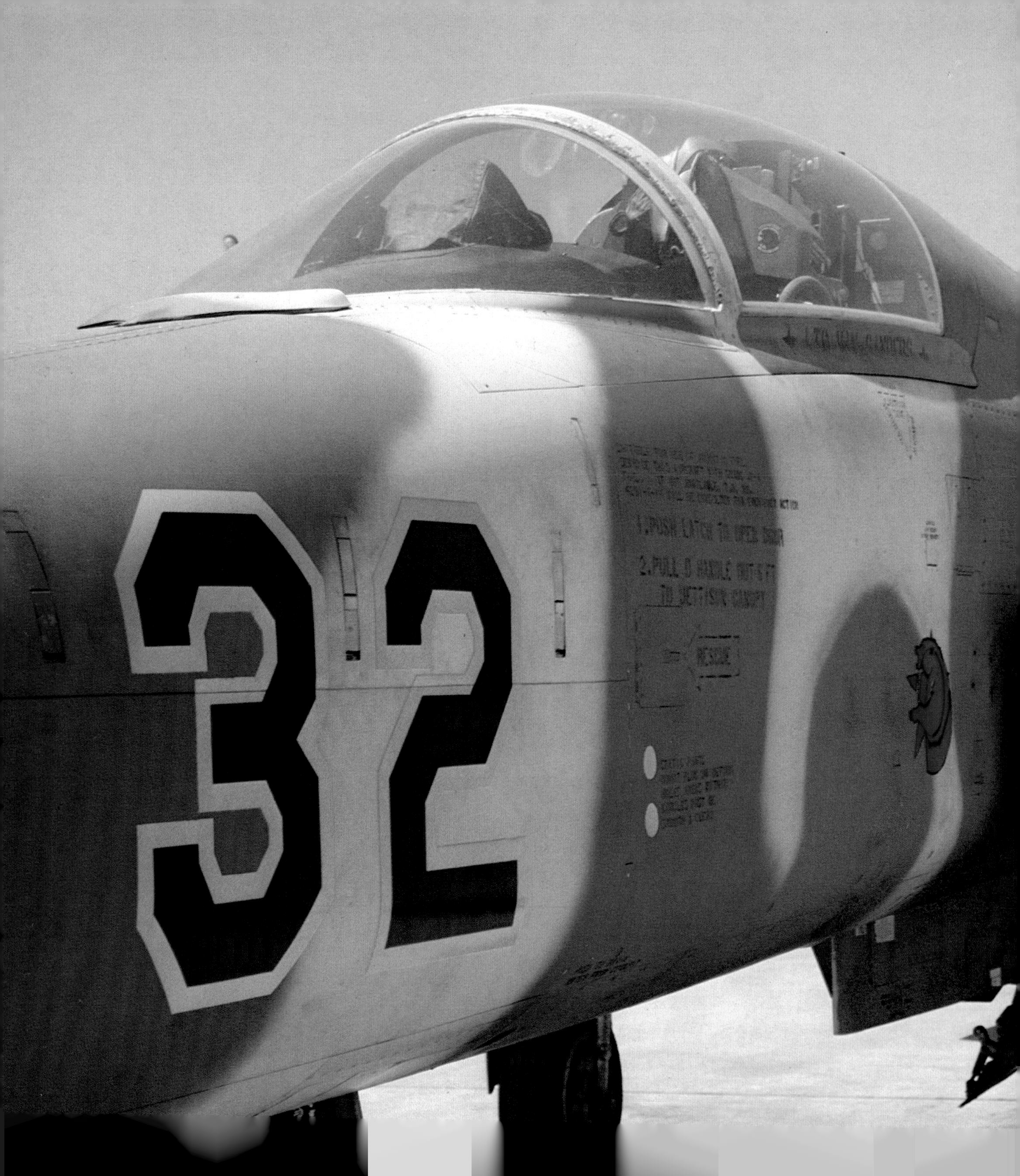

32
1.PUSH LATCH TO OPEN DOOR
RESCUE

F-5E Tiger IIs of the 527th Aggressor Squadron provide a realistic simulation of Soviet tactics in the air combat arena. The Tiger is sweet to handle, difficult to spot visually, and can 'pull lead' in the tightest of turns; its aerodynamic performance is broadly similar to most variants of the MiG-21. Deci is equipped with a computerized air combat manoeuvring installation (ACMI) to analyze and display all aircraft manoeuvres and claims during air combat training. Fighter controllers can 'kill remove' any 'dead' players during the course of an engagement

# Air superiority

Tornado F.2 ZD902/'AC' of No 229 OCU parked on the
ASP (aircraft servicing pan) at RAF Coningsby in
Lincolnshire. The Tornado ADV is the newest addition to
the RAF's front-line, some 165 aircraft (more may follow)
will provide long-range air defence for the UK. Striking
from beyond visual range with its combination of jam-
resistant Foxhunter radar and Sky Flash missiles, the F.2/3
force will be capable of destroying and disrupting large
formations of enemy strike aircraft

**Left** Two Tornado F.2s transit at low-level: the wings are
swept in the intermediate position (45 degrees). The F.3
will be fitted with auto-sweep (introduced on the F-14
Tomcat) to ensure the best lift/drag ratio is achieved in
combat manoeuvres

**Above** Tornado F.2s in echelon starboard: ZD932/'AM'
and ZD902/'AC' were pictured in May 1985 as the OCU
was working-up, before staff began training crews for the
first F.3 squadrons

**Following spread** A Bitburg-based F-15C takes the scenic route back to Deci along the Sardinian coastline. Interestingly, the jet nozzles are converged

Birds of a feather? An F-15C Eagle of the 36th Tactical Fighter Wing based at Bitburg in West Germany, in company with a Hawk during a formation recovery to Deci after a 2 v 2 v 2 fight against two Hawks and another pair of F-15s. Each aircraft carried an SN231 instrumentation pod (below) to feed the range computer with speed, height, G-loading, AOA, missile/gun status and range data

'Spike' Newbery, Pete John, and 'Ned' Kelly (extreme right) head for the de-brief after a combat with the Bitburg F-15s

The dream of most fighter pilots is to fly an F-15. Sitting in that cockpit he is probably in control of the most potent piece of air combat machinery in the world. Its advanced weapons system, raw power, phenomenal acceleration, and aerodynamic subtlety translate into the ability to out-manoeuvre any opponent and kill him, or disengage at will

Refuelling from a Victor K.2 (XL161) of No 55 Sqn at 25,000 ft (7620 m) over the North Sea. Operating procedures require the receiver to wait on the port side of the tanker, move astern to refuel, then clear to starboard. The performance of the receiver aircraft determines the height at which refuelling takes place

**Above right** Phantom FGR.2 (F-4M), XT914/'N' of No 228 OCU in trail behind the tanker, refuelling probe extended. The 'Tomb' forms the mainstay of Britain's air defences, and it remains a formidable aircraft. After the introduction of Tornado F.3s, four squadrons of Phantoms (two in West Germany) are being retained in the air combat role until deliveries of the European Fighter Aircraft (EFA) begin in the late 1990s

Pictured in March 1983, still wearing its naval uniform, this Ministry of Technology Phantom YF-4K2, XT596, was being used for RHAG (runway hydraulic arrestor gear) trials, flown by British Aerospace test pilot Geoff Peck. At the time I thought I'd flown through a time warp; the carrier *Ark Royal* catapulted her last Phantom in November 1978, and sailed-off to the scrap yard. The RN Phantom fleet was absorbed by the RAF

**Right** Whether combat manoeuvring or in the midst of a formation recovery, correct visual orientation is essential. A Sea Harrier slides into view—in combat its pilot would be in serious trouble

**Preceding pages** Two Sea Harrier FRS.1s of No 800 Sqn, Fleet Air Arm, based at RNAS Yeovilton in Somerset, outbound to the Loestock range for some practice bombing. Each aircraft dropped a dozen 4 kg bombs on this sortie

**Above** A somewhat dirty Sea Harrier displays CBLS pods on its centreline and wing pylons. During the Falklands conflict, Sea Harriers scored 24 kills for no loss in air combat

**Left** The bubble canopy and cockpit layout of the Sea Harrier are a major improvement over the RAF GR.3

**Above** A Lightning F.6 on the prowl in and around the deep Welsh valleys of Snowdonia. Only advanced pulsed-Doppler radars are capable of tracking a high speed target against terrain like this

**Left** Lightning F.3 'Delta Alpha' (XR749) of the Binbrook-based LTF, a unit which celebrated its 10th anniversary on 1 October 1985. Flown on this special occasion by Flt Lt Al 'Porky' Page, the aircraft is unusual in not having its serial number repeated under the wings

**Overleaf** The Binbrook QRA shed at sunrise: two F.6 Lightnings, fully armed and fuelled, are held at 10 minutes readiness. The night before this picture was taken, many hours were spent clearing the runway of snow and ice by using konsin and urea—a task delegated to the RAF engineers

89

'Clachy' (Flt Lt Neil Maclachlan) caught moments before he fired a Red Top missile from the port pylon of a Lightning T.5. A radar boot or visor covers the left-hand 'B' scope and one of the stowed ejection seat pins (labelled red) is visible on the cockpit coaming

**Overleaf** 'Delta Foxtrot' (nearest) and 'Delta Zulu', two Lightnings from the LTF, buster (accelerate to high speed)—a vital preparatory action before combat is joined. A lot of energy keeps your options open in a fight

'Fox Two': the Red Top accelerates away, guiding towards the target. After a meticulous briefing, Flt Lt Ian Howe captured this view of the launch from the right-hand seat

In this sequence of a Red Top launching from another Lightning T.5, the missile is still clearly visible, but the rocket motor soon burns out to give a tactically desirable smoke-free coast phase to the target. Although an old missile, the infrared homing Red Top deserves to be treated with respect; it's faster than most and the large 65 lb (29 kg) warhead ensures a high degree of terminal lethality

**Preceding pages** Sporting different colour schemes, a pair of Binbrook Lightnings from No 11 Sqn slake their thirst from the wing stations of a hemp camouflaged Victor K.2 (XH669) of No 232 OCU. Lightning jockeys operate daily with fuel reserves that make other fast-jet pilots shudder. If Binbrook's runway is rendered unusable (black), a crash diversion is flown to an airfield close to the parent base. The normal fuel uplift of a Lightning F.6 is around 9700 lb (4400 kg), which gives an endurance (to dry tanks) of 1 hour 30 minutes. A minimum of 1600 lb (727 kg) is required for a crash div, enough for 12 minutes' flying on one engine

**Overleaf** Lightning F.6 'Alpha Bravo' of No 5(F) Sqn cruising off the Lincolnshire coast. Missile rounds are usually carried without fins to minimize fatigue damage

Impromptu Lightning two-ship: the nearest aircraft, an F.6 (XP693), is employed by British Aerospace, while the camouflaged F.3 bears the name of Flt Lt Dave 'Frosty' Frost, tragically killed in West Germany in 1984 and one of the three Lightnings pilots to whom this book is dedicated

Sqn Ldr Dave Carden, a former flight commander with
No 5(F) Sqn, airborne during his 3000th Lightning hour

The office—Lightning F.6 cockpit

Once upon a time, not so long ago, RAF Lightnings regularly out-flew the fighters used by other NATO air forces. F-100s, F-104s, F-4s, and Mirages would sit squarely in their sights in combat after combat, their fate confirmed on gun camera film screened by gleeful pilots after landing back at base. The F-15 and F-16 changed all that. This Lightning F.6 of No 5(F) Sqn is being paced by a Belgian Air Force F-16 Fighting Falcon from No 349 *Smaldeel* (squadron), part of No 1 Wing based at Beauvechain

**Left** Even today, few aircraft can match the superlative climb performance of the Lightning; the initial climb rate of an F.6 is in the region of 50,000 ft (15,240 m) per minute. On being asked by ATC 'check your outbound heading' after departing an airfield off a practice approach, it's quite satisfying to come back with the reply, 'Vertical!'

**Overleaf** Captain De Vos Herman of No 349 Sqn off the starboard wing of my Lightning (visible at right of picture), before a 1 v 1 air combat with his F-16. After 5–6 minutes in full 'burner (I'd just air-to-air refuelled), pulling and pushing into $+6/-2G$ manoeuvres, I allowed myself the thought that I was doing better than OK against Herman's high-tech American hot rod. Then it happened. Herman suddenly zocked into my six, taking enough film for a couple of Hollywood movies.

Back on the ground, I asked 'Fox' (Herman's nickname) 'What did you do?—I mean, you came from nowhere.' Fox replied, 'Oh, I was finding it a bit difficult so I decided to use my afterburner. . .'

En route back to Beauvechain, Fox and his F-16 head for Mike Charlie 6, a mandatory reporting point on the fringe of the UK flight information region (FIR)

*Luftwaffe* Phantom F-4F (37–05) of JG-74 during a NATO exchange with the Lightnings of No 11 Sqn at Binbrook

**Overleaf** Glinting F-4F in a splash of evening sunshine

**Overleaf** French connection: *Armée de l'Air* Mirage F.1s of EC 1/30 based at Arienne-Reims

**Left** F-4F Phantom taxies past 5 Sqn and LTF Lightnings at Binbrook. JG-74 is normally based at Neuberg

**Below** West Germany purchased 175 F-4Fs, fitted with wing leading edge slats (pictured), but without Sparrow missiles and lacking (initially) in-flight refuelling capability. German Phantom crews are trained at George AFB in California

**Bottom** Curvy study of an F-4F at rest

Aircraft don't come any faster than the SR-71 Blackbird. The SR-71 operates above 99 per cent of the Earth's atmosphere, cruising at speeds in excess of 2100 mph (3380 km/h) to gather intelligence data with a variety of sophisticated sensors. Built by Lockheed's secret Skunk Works in beautiful downtown Burbank, the SR-71 is the product of a design genius—'Kelly' Johnson. His famous design axiom could also be applied to air combat tactics; KISS—'Keep it simple, stupid.' **Below** The scene is Mildenhall, home of Detachment 4, 9th Strategic Reconnaissance Wing, 1st Strategic Reconnaissance Squadron. A Blackbird crew prepare to 'snap in' at the beginning of a mission. To save time, all the external walkaround checks have already been completed, but around 45 minutes will elapse before the Blackbird swings onto the runway and kicks in the 'burners. **Right** Pulling away from the KC-135Q tanker after refuelling at 27,000 ft (8000 m) over the North Sea. For a five hour mission 'up North', the Blackbird will need a total of three air-to-air refuellings. **Overleaf** The Blackbird is crewed by a pilot (visible in pressure suit) and an RSO (Reconnaissance Systems Officer) in the back-seat. Two small side windows give the RSO a view of the outside world; he also has a periscope mounted under the forward fuselage to visually check the ground track for navigation purposes